A DYING BUSINESS:

A Comedy in Two Acts - Plus a Funeral

by

Mark de Castrique

Performance of A DYING BUSINESS is subject to a royalty.

First-class professional, stock, and amateur applications for performance permission or other production rights must be made in advance at mark@markdecastrique.com

ALSO BY MARK de CASTRIQUE

NOVELS
Dangerous Undertaking
Grave Undertaking
Foolish Undertaking
Final Undertaking
Fatal Undertaking
Risky Undertaking
Blackman's Coffin
The Fitzgerald Ruse
The Sandburg Connection
A Murder in Passing
A Specter of Justice
Hidden Scars
The 13th Target
The Singularity Race
Double Cross of Time
A Conspiracy of Genes
Death on a Southern Breeze
Available through all bookstores

A DYING BUSINESS: A Comedy in Two Acts, Plus a Funeral

Copyright 2005

Mark de Castrique

All Rights Reserved. No part of this publication may be reproduced, stored in, or introduced into a retrieval system, or transmitted in any form, or by any means (electronic, mechanical, photocopying, recording, or otherwise) without the prior written permission of the copyright owner and the publisher of this book.

MARK et al.

316 Robmont Rd.

Charlotte, NC 28270

mark@markdecastrique.com

A DYING BUSINESS:

A Comedy in Two Acts, Plus a Funeral

Characters:

LILY McADAMS - early 50s, wife of Horace McAdams, III.

HORACE McADAMS, III - early 50s, owner of McAdams & Son Funeral Directors.

BRENDA McADAMS - 16, self-conscious teenager embarrassed by her family's profession.

JOHN AGEE - late 70s, funeral home assistant and link to the past generations.

HORACE "ACE" McADAMS, IV - 20, student at Louisiana College of Mortuary Sciences in New Orleans.

PREACHER CHARLIE WINFIELD - 30s, Baptist preacher at Tabernacle of the Johns.

TONIA ROBERTS - 20s, African-American woman working in Buncombe County Social Services in Asheville, N.C. Granddaughter of deceased Ernie Roberts.

HATTIE ROBERTS - 70s, African-American spinster. Sister of deceased Ernie Roberts.

Setting: McAdams & Son Funeral Home in the small N.C. mountain town of Ridgetop.

Stage is set with two areas:

Stage Right, a kitchen;

Stage Left, a chapel suggested by cross, altar, and chairs.

Time: Three days - Monday, Tuesday, Wednesday in early December, 1999.

A DYING BUSINESS

ACT ONE

MONDAY MORNING

Scene 1

McAdams Funeral Home - Chapel

Curtain rises on darkened stage. A spotlight fades up as Narrator JOHN AGEE walks forward from the darkness and discovers the audience. JOHN AGEE is in his late 70s. He is dressed in clean work clothes and carrying a fishing pole. This fishing pole is his "narrator accessory" and is never present with his in-the-action wardrobe. JOHN is surprised, but not intimidated by the presence of the audience.

JOHN AGEE

Hello there... How y'all doin'?... Well, I'm doin' fine too... . Now I ain't much for talkin'... But, since y'all are here, and I'm passin' through, I'll say a word or two. Just take a moment of your time.

JOHN pauses, contemplating his own words.

JOHN AGEE (cont'd)

A moment ... You know, that's all any of us have ... a moment. If we're lucky, a string of moments ... one after the other, but with no guarantee we'll get that next one. Some of 'em ya catch and make the most of. (He casts the fishing pole without releasing line.) Some of 'em slip away never to be hooked again. I know. I've lost my share. By the way, my name's John Agee. I grew up in these mountains. Climbed ever ridge, fished ever stream. Some of y'all might know me from McAdams and Son Funeral Home. Started there in '45, right after the big one. Worked with Horace McAdams, Senior, down to Horace McAdams the Fourth.

Now, that's a lot of moments. In the funeral bidness, you hear about the special ones ... the eulogies pick out the best of the lot. We all should be makin' 'em ... special moments that we can relive, retell, or have others tell about us. And then there are them moments that should have been 'preciated at the time, but go unnoticed, makin' our stories . . . well, unfinished.

I need to share a couple – happened not too long ago. Some of ya may remember, though I don't recognize none of ya. Some of ya might recollect when Birdie Campbell died. In all my years, I never seen a woman's passin' create so many moments for so many people. Startin' with Mizz Lily and endin' with me. Well, I said I ain't much of a talker, but here I am ramblin' on when I ought to show ya. I mean y'all are sittin' down and facin' this way. It was a little before Christmas, the last Christmas of the century, Mizz Lily got a phone call one morning. Seems like nobody had a good word for the dearly departed Birdie Campbell, and the funeral was only two days off . . .

Lights fade up on LILY in next scene. Lights fade out on Narrator JOHN AGEE.

. . . but take a look and a listen for your own selves.

Scene 2

McAdams Funeral Home - Kitchen

LILY McADAMS is on the telephone. Receiver is corded to instrument on the wall and LILY is maneuvering the long spiral cord around set and other characters who enter. She is talking while setting out on the kitchen table three cereal bowls, a box of cereal, a half-gallon of milk, three glasses, and a carton of orange juice.

LILY

Helen, what do you mean you all decided? (listens) Duties of the office? I'd think that would fall under the . . . the social committee. (listens) Well, technically a funeral . .

HORACE McADAMS, III enters, looks askance at his wife, sits down and starts to fix his cereal.

LILY (cont'd)

. . . a funeral may not be a social function, but you said yourself the garden club will all sit together! (listens)

HORACE

Lily, there's no reserved seating except for family. You know that.

LILY waves him to be quiet.

LILY

What does Horace directing the funeral have to do with it?

HORACE looks at LILY with alarm.

LILY (cont'd)

Your husband owns a hardware store, but you don't make a speech to the customers when commode plungers go on sale. (listens) I'm sorry . . . I'm not comparing Birdie to a commode plunger . . . (listens and starts to weaken.) Yes, I know she was a forty-year member. (listens)

BRENDA McADAMS comes in carrying school books and dodging the phone cord. She is wearing tight jeans and pullover top with a bare midriff. HORACE looks disapprovingly at her. BRENDA sets her book bag on the floor and herself in a seat. She starts fixing her cereal.

LILY (cont'd)

Well, I guess as president I could make a few general remarks. (listens) No, not a eulogy, Helen, a few remarks, but I expect you or someone else to take care of the flowers. (listens) Oh, I don't know. Buy them out of the Christmas fund and we'll use the arrangement again at the luncheon next week. (listens) It's at eleven the day after tomorrow. (listens) Yes, Wednesday. Birdie's nephew is driving her sister up from Charlotte. (listens) Yes. Ten-thirty should insure you a good seat, Helen. (listens) Yes, goodbye.

LILY hangs up, sits down and starts eating.

BRENDA

Maybe we should think about selling tickets.

HORACE

Maybe you should think about wearing something that covers your belly button, young lady. Two weeks till Christmas and you look like you're headed to Myrtle Beach.

BRENDA

It's like the beach at school, Dad. Those old steam radiators . .

LILY

The same heating system when we were kids, Horace. You remember how hot those stuffy rooms got.

HORACE

Yes. The same as when my father went there, but you didn't see us walking around with our belly buttons hanging out.

LILY

Please, Horace, I'm eating

BRENDA

So, Mom, who was that on the phone so early?

LILY

Helen Walker. The Garden Club wants me to say something at Birdie Campbell's funeral.

BRENDA

Birdie the Biddy?

HORACE

Brenda, don't speak ill of the dead.

BRENDA

I've heard Mom say she'd like to strangle her.

LILY

That's just a figure of speech.

BRENDA

Oh, I see, you meant it in the good sense.

HORACE

What are you going to say, Lily?

LILY

I don't know. She was a forty-year member of the Garden Club, but she never did anything but complain.

HORACE

How about "Bye, bye, Birdie?"

LILY

Horace, you're no better than Brenda.

HORACE

Ridgetop is a small town. Surely she had friends who can give you some stories. Those always personalize a eulogy.

LILY

It's not a eulogy! It's a few remarks. And I don't know. Birdie got even more crusty in her old age. I think her closest friends are some of the Florida widows. They only have to be around her in the summer.

BRENDA

She get any flowers yet?

HORACE

Good idea. I believe a few have arrived. John will know. You can check who sent them and give 'em a call.

LILY

And you can drive Brenda to school. Between Birdie's funeral and Ace coming home today, I'm running out of time.

HORACE

All right, but, Brenda, you either change clothes or I'm taking you there in the hearse.

BRENDA

Geez, Mom!

LILY

This is not the battle to pick, dear.

BRENDA gets up from the table.

BRENDA

I wish I had my own car.

HORACE

Well, we're getting a new hearse next year. I'll keep you in mind for the old one.

BRENDA rolls her eyes and exits.

LILY

Horace, you should be more sensitive.

HORACE

About what?

LILY

About Brenda's feelings. She's at the age when she's embarrassed about living here.

HORACE

A lot of families in this town live where they work.

LILY

But how many have caskets and corpses in their back room?

HORACE

Lily, that's not fair! This is an honorable business. Has been for over eighty years, and soon Ace will continue that tradition. Nothing has changed.

LILY

Brenda has changed, Horace. She's sixteen, she's unsure of herself, and she's interested in boys.

HORACE

Boys?

LILY

Yes, boys. She's a teenage girl.

HORACE

But she goes out on dates.

LILY

A few. And how many of them ever pick her up here?

HORACE

Well, there's . . . uh, there must be . . . oh, I don't know how many.

LILY

Zero. She always arranges to be over at Cindy's or Sharon's.

HORACE

Then maybe I need to talk to her. You're not Morticia and I'm not Gomez.

LILY

No, we're the "MacAddams" Family.

She hums first few bars of Addams Family TV theme song "do do do do" and snaps fingers. HORACE joins her on repeat.

LILY (cont'd)

And don't tell me that didn't bother you. We went out ten times before you invited me to this house.

HORACE

Well, what am I supposed to do?

LILY

Cut her a little slack. She's a good kid. Maybe we could let her throw a party here. For New Year's. Ace could help. She adores her brother.

HORACE

Maybe. Though Ace and I have a lot to talk about. We've got a partnership to work out.

LILY

He's not going to want to spend his Christmas break talking funeral business.

HORACE

But he graduates this Spring. He'll be taking on responsibilities.

LILY

Don't assume too much, Horace. He may have his own ideas. Now you'd better get Brenda to school. And no more teasing about the hearse.

HORACE

I'll be the silent chauffeur. I'll even drive without the headlights on. You just worry about Birdie.

LILY

Oh, God, don't remind me. You think she could have lived till after New Year's when I'm no longer president. But, no, not Birdie. She had to get me one last time. I wish she weren't dead so I could strangle her.

BLACK OUT

Scene 3

McAdams Funeral Home – Chapel

Lights up on JOHN AGEE in Chapel. He is dressed in work clothes different from scene 1. He is setting out greenery from a cardboard box and arranging a few bouquets amidst the ferns, holly, and shiny galax. He is half-humming, half-singing "Shall We Gather At The River."

LILY enters carrying a notepad.

LILY

Good Morning, John.

JOHN

Mornin', Mizz McAdams.

LILY

Aren't you setting these arrangements out early? Birdie's funeral isn't until Wednesday.

JOHN

Just doin' some planning. Don't think ol' Birdie will be gettin' many flowers so I thought I'd best see what we can put together so it don't look too skimpy. Don't want it to reflect poorly on the funeral home. I'll put 'em back in the chiller when I'm through.

LILY

You're using holly?

JOHN

Yep. Festive ain't it. For the season. Cut it myself. And the fact that it's prickly fits the ol' biddy.

LILY

John, not you too. I'd think after working here over fifty years you'd be more respectful.

JOHN

Seen 'em come, seen 'em go. And ain't goin' to remember 'em the way they ain't. John Agee ain't no hypocrite. You can make your speech however you want, that's your bidness.

LILY

Speech - How'd you know about the speech?

JOHN

It's Monday. Time for my two-week haircut; so I was in the barbershop at eight this morning. It was the talk of both chairs.

LILY

That Helen Walker! She hadn't even asked me yet. The ol' biddy.

JOHN

Yep. She's another one.

LILY

Well, it's not a speech . . . And just who are you calling a hypocrite?

JOHN

All right. You got the privilege to say what you're goin' to say, Mizz McAdams. Whether you believe it or not.

LILY

Yes. I do. Now which of these arrangements came with cards?

LILY kneels down in front of a hodgepodge of carnations and reads card.

LILY (cont'd)

"In Memory of Birdie: When the time came for her to pass, We hope she had a tank of gas. - The Boys at Mort's Texaco."

JOHN

There's a greasy thumbprint to prove it.

LILY moves over to a larger, more professionally done arrangement.

LILY

Now here's a nice one. (She reads card.) "Tabernacle of the Johns Baptist Church." She was a life-long active member.

"Birdie has come to the end of her story,

And in God's love she abides.

We give Him all the praise and glory

For moving her on to the other side."

JOHN

Truer words of faith were never spoken.

LILY

John, I think I can manage without your help. This is a good lead. I'm sure Reverend Winfield can give me some ideas.

LILY moves to another bouquet and reads card.

LILY (cont'd)

"For Birdie - she leaves the world a better place. - The Cardinal Cafe."

JOHN

Now there's a bird cage for you. I can hear them cronies cacklin' at the back table now. If you ain't there talkin', you're being talked about.

LILY

Yes, John. Sounds a lot like the barbershop, doesn't it.

LILY looks around.

LILY (cont'd)

Is this all?

JOHN

So far. Mabel at the floral shop said she's makin' up a big one from Birdie's sister that was wired out of Charlotte. She won't have that ready till tomorrow. I expect we'll get a few more. See why I'm addin' our own stock?

LILY

Yes.

JOHN looks at the overall presentation.

JOHN

Think I'll work on a wreath. We got her embalmed last night so I got time on my hands . . . unless we're lucky enough to get another one.

LILY

Do me a favor, John. Don't wish for that kind of luck. I'm going to make some calls. Horace will be back in a few minutes. He ran Brenda to school.

JOHN

I'll just finish up here, then put these flowers in with Birdie.

LILY

Let me know if any others come in.

JOHN

Whatever you say, Mizz McAdams. Oh, is Ace coming in today?

LILY

Yes. He's driving all night from Louisiana. Don't count on him for any help. He'll probably go straight to bed.

JOHN

You know I was about Ace's age when I first started working for your husband's grandfather, Horace Sr. Then Horace Jr., then Horace the Third, and, good Lord willing, a few years with your Ace. I tell you, Mizz McAdams, I think Ace is the brightest bulb in the family chandelier.

LILY

Ace thinks a lot of you too, John. He really does.

JOHN nods, more to himself than to LILY.

JOHN

Well, you'd best be about your Birdie bidness. I'll make sure you'll be standin' up here in a display that suits you both.

LILY exits.

JOHN goes back to the cardboard box and begins extracting lengths of fake Christmas greenery. Some of it has Christmas lights attached to it. He picks up softly singing "Peace Like A River."

HORACE enters carrying a thin, 2-foot-square box under his arm. He sees John working and sets down the box.

HORACE

John, what are you doing?

JOHN

Helpin' Mizz McAdams.

HORACE

Helping her do what?

JOHN

Why, set the stage for her speech. You know about the speech, don't you?

HORACE

Oh, yes, but you'd better call it "a few remarks."

JOHN

We don't think Birdie's goin' to get too many flowers. I was pullin' some stock greenery, what with her sister coming up from Charlotte and all. I know Ace ain't goin' to be able to help you today after drivin' all night.

HORACE

That's true. You know, John, six more months and Ace can start taking the load off both of us. You might even think of retiring.

JOHN

Retiring? To do what? Wait around till I wind up in the back room? Till I come back as bidness?

HORACE

I just thought since you're 77 . . .

JOHN

76

HORACE

. . .77 next month, you'd want to take it easy. While you've still got your health.

JOHN

I got my health cause I come in here every day since I was twenty-two. I slow down, ol' death'll catch me for sure. I ain't ready, I tell you.

HORACE

You're not superstitious, are you, that working on the dead keeps you alive?

JOHN

That's the dumbest thing I ever heard. Breathin' keeps you alive. That's the difference. Old or young, rich or poor, good health or bad health, all of 'em in the back room got one thing in common: they ain't breathin'. The most natural thing for me next to breathin' is workin'. So, if I stop workin', what's the next thing to go?

HORACE

Breathing.

JOHN

Exactly. Your wattage just went up in the chandelier.

HORACE

My wattage?

JOHN

Never ya mind. I got to finish and get these blossoms in the chiller. Mizz McAdams is counting on me, and where Birdie's concerned, I don't think she can count on much else.

HORACE

Come over here. I want to show you something.

JOHN

Hold up. I'm just about finished.

HORACE

No. Ace may be here any minute. I want to show you his Christmas present.

JOHN

A surprise?

HORACE

Yes. I had Fletcher Monuments make it. Just picked it up after I dropped Brenda at school. Ace is going to love it.

HORACE sets the box on the floor and opens one end. He pulls out a bronze plaque and reads the inscription.

HORACE (cont'd)

McAdams & Son Funeral Directors: Founder - Horace McAdams, Sr. 1895 – 1957. You know, Ace's great granddaddy.

JOHN

I thought the name sounded familiar.

HORACE

Horace McAdams, Jr. 1918 – 1985

JOHN

Let me guess. That's your dad.

HORACE

Come on, John. This is important.

Then me, Horace McAdams, III. 1945 –

JOHN

And still breathin'.

HORACE

And Ace. Horace McAdams, IV. 1980 –

Well, what do you think?

JOHN

Y'all goin' in one grave?

HORACE

No. It's a commemorative plaque for outside the chapel. It will be a comfort to the families.

JOHN

A comfort?

HORACE

Yes. That there's always been a Horace McAdams for their time of need.

JOHN

How 'bout a small plaque beside this one. John Agee 1923 and unretired. Been there for the time of need of four generations of Horace McAdamses.

JOHN picks up the last arrangement of flowers and walks off. HORACE looks after him, surprised at the reaction.

BLACK OUT

Scene 4

McAdams Funeral Home – Kitchen

(Lights up.)

LILY McADAMS is on the telephone.

LILY

Yes, God bless you too. Is Reverend Winfield in? (listens) Oh, when do you expect him? (listens) Can I leave a message? (listens) Please ask him to call Lily McAdams at . . . (interruption/pause) He did? He said he was coming here? (listens) No, no, that's perfect. And you're sure he said he wanted to talk to me about Birdie Campbell? (listens) Yes, Yes, praise His name. (She hangs up) Yes!

BLACK OUT

Scene 5

McAdams Funeral Home - Chapel

Lights up

HORACE is sitting on steps of the altar, looking at the plaque and thinking.

ACE

(off stage)

Dad – Mom - I'm home!

HORACE

Ace! I'm in the chapel.

HORACE stands up and starts to go meet his son, then remembers the plaque is out of the box. He hurries back and just slides it in as ACE enters. ACE is wearing jeans, running shoes, and a heavy sweatshirt with "LOUISIANA COLLEGE OF MORTUARY SCIENCES" on the front and "FIGHTING ZOMBIES" on the back. He gives HORACE a hug, then looks around the chapel.

ACE

What are you doing?

HORACE

Preparing for Birdie Campbell's funeral.

ACE looks again at the bare chapel.

ACE

Why isn't John helping?

HORACE

He did. The funeral's not till day after tomorrow. John pulled some greenery out of storage to see if we had enough. He's just putting it back.

ACE

Where's Mom?

HORACE

Probably on the phone. She's giving the eulogy for Birdie.

ACE

Mom?

HORACE

Yes. But call it "a few remarks."

ACE

Brenda at school?

HORACE

Brenda's growing up, Ace.

ACE

Yeah, sixteen going on twenty-five.

HORACE

No. I mean growing up . . . and away. We embarrass her. This place . . . the business.

ACE

Aw, it's just a stage, Dad.

HORACE

A stage?

ACE

She'll grow through it. She knows you and Mom are what make it home.

HORACE

Of course, it's home. I mean it's not her funeral home.

ACE

What if she wants to go into the business?

HORACE

Brenda? A woman undertaker? Even if she is a McAdams, that's just not going to happen.

ACE

Why not?

HORACE

I mean . . . maybe a child, or a woman, but I can't see your sister embalming a man.

ACE

But there will be women in my graduating class.

HORACE

Well, they're not coming to work in Ridgetop, North Carolina. Now if Brenda wants to marry someone in the business, that's fine. Who knows? With Ridgetop growing like it is . . . with all the retirees flocking to the mountains and dying, we could maybe support another employee . . . even a minor partner.

HORACE looks down at the boxed plaque.

HORACE (cont'd)

If John retires . . . someday.

ACE

Dad, I just asked if Brenda's at school.

HORACE

Yes. Her Christmas break starts Wednesday. And everything is going to be fine, son. Now that you're home.

ACE starts off-stage.

ACE

Well, I gotta go.

HORACE

Go? You just got here.

ACE halts.

ACE

I gave Ernie Roberts a ride from school.

HORACE

There's another student from here?

ACE

No. He manages the college laundry.

HORACE

At LCMS?

ACE

Small world, huh. His sister's lived here for years. Hattie Roberts. Black woman. Ernie said she retired from the high school cafeteria about ten years ago . . . before Brenda and I went there.

HORACE thinks for several seconds.

HORACE

Miss Hattie. Yes . . . I remember her. She was there when your mother and I were in school.

ACE

Ernie grew up here. When he was a teenager, he went to Birmingham where jobs were better. Then he moved to New Orleans and got on at the college in the 70s. Now he's in his 70s, but he doesn't want to retire.

HORACE

Hmm. Heard that before. Where is he?

ACE

Sleeping in the car. I just dropped in to let you and Mom know I made it before I run him out to his sister's.

HORACE

Don't you want to rest? You've been driving all night.

ACE

Dad, it's just out Bear Creek road. I'll be back in thirty minutes.

PREACHER CHARLIE WINFIELD enters, wearing winter coat.

WINFIELD

Horace – there you are.

HORACE

Good morning, Preacher. You know Ace.

WINFIELD

Oh, yes. The son in McAdams & Son.

ACE

(uncomfortable)

Well, Reverend Winfield, it's really not . . .

HORACE

. . . it's really not official till Spring. But, I already think of him as my partner.

WINFIELD

And bringing in business already.

ACE

What business?

WINFIELD

Why, isn't that your Camaro out front? The one with the dead man in it? I tapped on the window and said "Praise The Lord," and when he didn't answer, I noticed his eyes wide open.

HORACE and ACE are dumbfounded.

WINFIELD (cont'd)

How'd you get him in there? . . . Slide him off a chair?

ACE bolts off-stage; HORACE follows.

WINFIELD stands bewildered for a few seconds, exits.

BLACK OUT

Scene 6

McAdams Funeral Home - Kitchen

Lights up

LILY McADAMS is on the phone.

LILY

Mort. It's Lily McAdams. (listens) Yes, I'm fine. (listens) No, the hearse didn't break down again. I'm calling about the flowers you and the boys at the station sent for Birdie. (listens) No, I didn't know they were recycled. Well, I hope you and your wife had a lovely anniversary. (listens) No, honest Mort, they look fresh as a daisy. (listens) Yes, I know they're carnations. Look, Mort, I was calling to see if you had any special memories of Birdie. (listens) Oh, you heard? (listens) No, just a few general remarks, but I'd like them to be as personal as possible. I wouldn't mention your name, just say a friend . . . (pause for interruption). . .oh, it was strictly a business gesture? (listens) Well, I don't know if you can write off the anniversary flowers, you'll have to ask your accountant.

ACE rushes in.

ACE

Mom. I need the phone. It's an emergency.

LILY

Oh, Mort, Ace just got home. I've got to go (listens) Yes, the funeral's Wednesday at eleven. (listens) Yes, Mort, I'll say you were there, but I doubt you'll be audited.

LILY hangs up.

LILY (cont'd)

Ace. Welcome home.

LILY starts to give ACE a hug, but he grabs the phone.

LILY (cont'd)

Ace?

ACE

Oh, Mom, it's terrible.

LILY

What? What?

ACE
(on the phone)

A medical emergency at McAdams Funeral Home. We're applying CPR but I'm afraid the man's dead. (listens) Yes, a dead man at the funeral home. (listens) No, this is not a joke. We need the EMTs immediately. (listens) This is Horace McAdams the Fourth, that's who. Just get here.

ACE hangs up.

LILY

Is it your father? John?

ACE

No. Ernie Roberts.

LILY

Who?

ACE

I just thought he went to sleep. I could have taken him to a hospital.

LILY

A student?

ACE

An elderly black man. He rode home with me.

LILY

To stay with us?

ACE

To spend Christmas with his sister, Hattie Roberts.

LILY

Miss Hattie from the cafeteria?

ACE

Yes.

LILY

Did he complain about anything?

ACE

No. About a half hour ago, he said he was real tired. He sighed and laid his head against the window.

LILY

Oh, Ace.

LILY gives ACE a mother's "welcome home" hug.

LILY (cont'd)

There's no way you could have known. He probably just went gently. Maybe that's why he was coming home.

ACE

Maybe . . . maybe he sensed something. It's kinda funny.

LILY

What?

ACE

He told me he was coming home for a funeral. Birdie Campbell's.

LILY

Birdie's? Did he say why?

ACE

No. You know what people thought of Birdie. Maybe he wanted to make sure she was dead. Well, I'd better help Dad. I guess one of us will have to call Ernie Roberts' sister.

ACE exits.

LILY

(to herself)

Coming back to Birdie's funeral . . . I wonder why.

BLACK OUT

Scene 7

McAdams Funeral Home - Chapel

Lights up

PREACHER WINFIELD enters. He nervously looks around the chapel for a few seconds.

WINFIELD

Lily? Lily?

JOHN AGEE enters.

JOHN

You lookin' for Mizz McAdams?

WINFIELD is startled.

WINFIELD

Yes. She's the reason I dropped by . . . before this unfortunate incident.

JOHN

I guess that's one way of puttin' it. I reckon she's in the kitchen on the phone about Birdie Campbell's unfortunate incident.

WINFIELD

Could you let her know I'm here?

JOHN

Yep. I could. Things settled down?

WINFIELD

The EMTs took Mr. Roberts to Foley Memorial where they'll pronounce him officially dead. I called Reverend Cal Stevens at AME Zion Church to see if he knew the sister. Turns out Hattie Roberts is one of his members. He can break the news in person.

JOHN

Always better.

WINFIELD

Ace wants to go too. He's going to pick Stevens up. The boy's taking it kinda hard.

JOHN

Didn't you tell him it was an "unfortunate incident?"

WINFIELD

No, you'd think he'd be used to it, growing up here.

JOHN

"It?" Used to "it?"

WINFIELD

"It." . . . You know, death.

JOHN

Preacher, I thought you'd know eventually we're all gonna get used to "it." We're all gonna be six-feet-under someday. It's other people's dyin' that's the problem. We don't do funerals for the dead; we do 'em for the living. You may get used to "breakin' the news," but I don't think anyone gets used to learnin' their loved one is dead.

WINFIELD

No. No, they don't.

JOHN

And I sure as hell hope you ain't one of them preachers who tell them God needed their mother, brother, wife, husband, or little child more than they did.

WINFIELD

I try to give them comfort and I pray for God to give them peace.

JOHN

Then maybe you'll amount to somethin', preacher. (JOHN winks at WINFIELD) I'll get Mizz McAdams.

LILY enters.

LILY

Get me for what?

                          WINFIELD

Lily, I want to talk with you about Birdie Campbell . . . if you have the time.

                            LILY

Yes, Reverend Winfield. Certainly.

LILY looks at JOHN and the inconvenient chapel seating.

                        LILY (cont'd)

Why don't we talk in the kitchen.

LILY and WINFIELD exit.

JOHN starts softly singing to himself "When The Roll Is Called Up Yonder."

BLACK OUT

Scene 8

McAdams Funeral Home   - Kitchen

Lights up

LILY leads WINFIELD in.

                            LILY

Sit where you're most comfortable, Reverend Winfield.

WINFIELD sits at kitchen table.

                          WINFIELD

This is fine. And please call me Charlie.

LILY sits at table beside him.

                            LILY

Well, Reverend Charlie, I'm just so thankful you came by.

                          WINFIELD

And let me say what a Godsend you are. I can handle the Order of Service, but the personal reflection you can offer will truly be a fitting memorial.

LILY

Actually, that's the problem. I'm only supposed to make a few remarks, but I don't have enough to say for even that. I'm hoping you can offer some suggestions, some anecdote that will set the right tone.

WINFIELD

Oh, dear.

LILY

Oh, dear, what?

WINFIELD

I'm afraid Birdie Campbell never warmed up to me. In fact, I've been told she led the opposition to my being called.

LILY

Really?

WINFIELD

Nothing personal I understand. She wanted an older, single preacher. She felt he would be more attentive to the senior members of the congregation.

LILY

More like your predecessor, Reverend Logan.

WINFIELD

No. Actually she didn't like Reverend Logan either.

LILY

She didn't?

WINFIELD

Lily, you're not Baptist.

LILY

Presbyterian.

WINFIELD

Yes, a nice orderly denomination. You see, Lily, every Baptist Church has two factions: those who believe their preacher is on fire for the Lord, and those who believe the Lord wants their preacher fired. Birdie Campbell was one of those dear souls who helps preachers relocate.

LILY

Oh, dear. I can't say that.

WINFIELD

If thou canst say something nice, thou shalt say nothing at all.

LILY

The Sermon on the Mount? Matthew?

WINFIELD

The Gospel According to Thumper. Bambi. Lily, when I can't say somethin' nice, silent prayer is mighty handy.

BLACK OUT

Scene 9

McAdams Funeral Home - Chapel

Lights up

ACE is arranging some silk flowers in a small basket on the altar table. Extra greenery lies beside it. ACE has changed into a collared shirt, dark slacks, and a navy blue sport coat. His hair is neatly combed.

JOHN AGEE enters.

JOHN

Most of the other silk flowers ain't appropriate. I was plannin' to use them for Birdie.

ACE

These will be fine, John. I just don't want to go over there empty-handed.

JOHN

She'll want to know about the trip.

ACE

The trip?

JOHN

The drive from New Orleans. You were the last person to talk to her brother . . . to see him alive.

ACE

Well, there's not much to tell. We talked about music. He played trumpet with some old-timers in New Orleans . . . just for fun. They called themselves "Jasmine Jazz Men," you know, first word's the flower Jasmine, then Jazz and Men. Mostly we talked about the college. He was concerned because they were pressuring him to retire.

JOHN

Ernie was only in his 70s.

ACE

Did you know him?

JOHN

We'd run into each other fishin'. . . when we were kids. Usually at Stony Pond. Weren't many of the coloreds up in the mountains back then.

ACE

African-Americans.

JOHN

The Ernie I knew was colored. And he didn't know anything more about Africa than I did. But he did know a lot about fishin'. Showed me the best spots. Yep, I liked him. I liked to gone fishin' with him . . . one last time.

ACE

Did you know his sister?

JOHN

Hattie?

He pauses to think but doesn't directly answer.

JOHN (cont'd)

She was a year or two younger. But, like I said, she'll want to know about the trip. So, don't leave her troubled.

ACE

Troubled?

JOHN

About the college . . . the retirement. Tell her a story if you have to. What good is the truth if it don't give comfort? (John thinks to himself a few seconds.) And who's to say otherwise? Ace, I done your mom a disservice. She's goin' to speak about Birdie Campbell, but she's goin' to be speakin' to Birdie's sister. She should say what she needs to make her happy.

ACE

And you knew Mr. Roberts, John. You want to come with us?

JOHN

To tell Hattie? No. You go. Take them flowers . . . but it's the story you tell that she'll remember.

ACE looks the arrangement over again, then takes a white card and pen out of his coat pocket. He starts to write a message.

JOHN picks up the unused greenery and flowers.

TONIA ROBERTS enters. She is an African-American woman in her early 20s. Sleek, sexy, a career woman, she wears stylish winter coat and carries a small floral arrangement of galax, baby's breath, and holly berries.

TONIA

Excuse me. Are either of you with the funeral home?

ACE and JOHN look at each other. JOHN steps back to let ACE answer.

ACE

Yes. I'm Ace McAdams.

TONIA

I brought some flowers for Miss Campbell.

ACE

I'll take care of them.

ACE sets his own arrangement back on the table and walks over to her.

> ACE (cont'd)
>
> Do you work for a floral shop?

ACE takes the flowers from her and sets them beside his.

> TONIA
>
> No. I'm bringing these from my aunt . . . my great aunt actually.

> ACE
>
> Oh, were she and Birdie old friends?

> TONIA
>
> I don't know. Aunt Hattie called me over the weekend and asked if I could pick these up. She arranged them herself. I live in Asheville, but I drop by to help her with errands and grocery shopping.

> ACE
>
> Aunt Hattie? Hattie Roberts?

> TONIA
>
> Yes. You know her?

ACE glances at JOHN. JOHN stays silent.

> ACE
>
> No, I'm afraid I don't. Did your aunt come with you?

> TONIA
>
> No. My grandfather's coming in from New Orleans. She wanted to be there when he arrives.

> ACE
>
> I need to talk with you, Miss . . .

ACE hangs the sentence out, not knowing her name.

> TONIA
>
> Roberts. Tonia Roberts.

ACE

Miss Roberts.

ACE looks at JOHN.

JOHN

I've got to put these away.

JOHN exits.

TONIA

What's wrong? Tell me what's wrong.

ACE

I gave your grandfather a ride.

TONIA

Granddaddy's here?

ACE

No. He's . . . he's not.

TONIA

But I came straight from Aunt Hattie's. Did I pass him on the way?

ACE

Your grandfather . . . your grandfather died. I just ran in here for a few moments. I thought he was sleeping.

ACE stops, not knowing what to say. TONIA just looks at him, unable to speak.

ACE (cont'd)

I thought he was sleeping. I'm so sorry.

TONIA

Dead? He's dead? You left him in the car? . . . in December? It's freezing outside.

ACE

Just for a few moments. The car was warm.

TONIA

You didn't even invite him inside? You wouldn't leave a dog in the car, but you left him.

ACE

Just for a few moments. He was facing away from me. I thought he was sleeping.

TONIA

Where is he? Where's my grandfather?

ACE

At the hospital. I called the medics, but it was too late. I'll drive you.

TONIA

I don't think so. You've done enough already.

TONIA glares at ACE as she fights conflicting emotions of anger and grief.

BLACK OUT

Scene 10

McAdams Funeral Home - Chapel

Lights fade up

Narrator JOHN AGEE is standing at the edge of chapel.

JOHN

No, not all memorable moments are happy ones. You heard me tell the Preacher the funeral bidness ain't about death, it's about the loss of a life . . . the loss to the living. . . . So, Monday ended on sad notes. Ace struggled with guilt that Ernie Roberts died right beside him – though I can tell ya even though I hadn't seen Ernie in 60 years, he never had a vengeful bone in his body and surely didn't carry no ill feelin's about Ace into the hereafter; Mizz Lily was still tryin' to find a good story about Birdie Campbell; and you remember Horace the Third and Brenda were having a father-daughter spat that I've got the good sense to stay out of.

But Monday was nothing compared to Tuesday when even I, a man who prides himself on mindin' his own bidness, even I had to . . . Well, here I go yappin' at ya again.

Lights fade up on next scene. Lights fade out on JOHN AGEE

> JOHN (cont'd)

It was in the kitchen, Tuesday morning, and Ace was about to turn things ever which way but loose.

TUESDAY MORNING

Scene 11

McAdams Funeral Home - Kitchen

LILY McADAMS in wardrobe change is setting out four cereal bowls, box of cereal, half gallon of milk, four glasses and a carton of orange juice.

ACE in wardrobe change enters. He sits at the table.

> ACE

Morning, Mom

> LILY

Ace. What are you doing up? I thought you'd sleep in.

> ACE

I couldn't. I kept seeing Tonia Roberts' face when I told her about her grandfather. I know she questions whether I did everything I could.

> LILY

That's only natural. Shock . . . disbelief . . . anger . . . sorrow. I'm sure she'll understand when she's had a chance to go through the grieving process.

> ACE

But I don't want her to think there was anything racial.

> LILY

Racial?

> ACE

Yeah. She believes I didn't pay attention to her grandfather. Ignored him.

LILY

But you gave him a ride out of kindness.

ACE

I want to do something more, Mom. The man died right beside me.

LILY

Like what?

ACE

I want to handle the funeral arrangements . . . at no charge. I mean at least at our cost for the casket and vault. Then I will have gotten him home . . . in a sense.

LILY

Have you asked Miss Hattie yet?

ACE

No. I'm going to call this morning and see if they'll come over.

LILY

Have you asked your father?

ACE

Not yet. I can't believe Dad would have a problem with it.

HORACE enters, followed by BRENDA. BRENDA is wearing a winter coat buttoned to the neck. She immediately sits down at the table.

HORACE

What problem?

ACE

(dodging the question)

Brenda, are you cold?

HORACE and LILY look at BRENDA.

BRENDA

Just a little chill.

HORACE

Well, it's warm enough in here. At least take your coat off while you eat. We aren't on a camping trip.

HORACE continues to stand, convinced that BRENDA is concealing another bare midriff. BRENDA gets up and takes off her coat. She is wearing a blouse tucked in her jeans.

BRENDA

What's the matter, Dad? Too revealing? Should I put my coat back on?

ACE

Little sister, I can see I'm going to have to keep the boys away from here with a stick.

BRENDA

Who are you kidding? You think anyone wants to go out with the Bride of Frankenstein?

BRENDA bursts into tears and runs offstage.

ACE

What . . . what'd I say? I don't think she's the Bride of Frankenstein.

LILY

It's not what you think. It's what she thinks. I'll go talk to her.

LILY exits.

HORACE

Son, that's what I was trying to tell you yesterday. It's like walking on eggshells around here. You were always . . . always more accepting. That's why you're ready to fit right in. I just don't understand Brenda.

ACE

I think it's harder on girls, Dad. From clothes, to friends, it's just a bigger deal.

HORACE

Well, your mother can calm her down. But what's this problem you were talking about?

ACE

Problem?

HORACE

When I came in, you were saying, "I can't believe Dad would have a problem with it." So what is "it."

ACE

A service for Ernie Roberts for free.

HORACE

Free! At our funeral home?

ACE

Well, maybe not free, but for cost . . . our hard costs.

HORACE

Son, they're a black family.

ACE

So, what's that got to do with it? If death doesn't discriminate, why should you?

HORACE

I'm not discriminating. The man happened to die in your car. You feel responsible. You're not, but if you want to help the family . . . help Miss Hattie, that's fine with me. Just don't be surprised.

ACE

Surprised? Surprised at what?

HORACE

Surprised if they say no.

ACE

Because they're mad at me?

HORACE

No, because they're black and this is a white funeral home. Neither one of us can change that.

ACE is angry. He gets up from the table.

####### ACE

So that's it. They're black and we're a white . . . a lily white funeral home. Well, you're wrong. And there will be change, one way or the other, Dad. I can promise you that.

ACE exits.

####### HORACE

Oh, come on, Ace.

HORACE sighs. Throws down his napkin. Gets up and follows his son.

BLACK OUT

Scene 12

McAdams Funeral Home – Kitchen

BRENDA sits at the kitchen table. She has stopped crying, except for the occasional tear wiped from her cheek.

LILY steps tentatively into the room.

####### LILY

Brenda? What are you doing back in the kitchen?

####### BRENDA
(not looking at her)

Nothing.

####### LILY

Then why are you in here crying?

####### BRENDA
(sobbing again)

I can't find a pencil for school.

LILY walks to a kitchen drawer and lifts out several new pencils.

####### LILY

Here's a whole box full.

####### BRENDA

I can't find a pencil without McAdams Funeral Home stamped on it.

LILY

What's this really about, Brenda?

BRENDA

I said nothing.

LILY

Nothing? Your brother pays you a compliment and you burst into tears? What boy is this "nothing" about?

BRENDA

Chris Murphy.

LILY

The basketball Chris Murphy? What did he do to upset you?

BRENDA

He asked me out.

LILY

I admit I'm out of touch, but when a boy asked me out, especially the star of the high school team, I was usually happy.

BRENDA

Out's not so bad. He asked to come over here tomorrow. We're doing a history project over the break and he wants to study together. But, Mom, I think he really likes me.

LILY

And you're embarrassed for him to come to the funeral home.

BRENDA starts crying again. LILY sits down beside her.

LILY (cont'd)

There's no reason to be embarrassed by what your father does or where we live. I accepted it when I started going out with him. You make no big deal about it. If it bothers Chris, confront it, laugh about it, and talk about other things. We don't have bodies falling out of closets. The boy said he wanted to come over. He's obviously not expecting Bela Lugosi to answer the door.

BRENDA

But it was easier for you and Dad.

LILY

Would you believe your father use to be self-conscious too? But I liked him and took the bull by the horns.

BRENDA

Really? What did you do?

LILY

Well, I thought he liked me in high school. The same feeling you have about Chris Murphy. But your father was too shy to ask me out, and back then girls just had to wait.

BRENDA

So, what happened?

LILY

Well, I waited and waited, but nothing happened. Then we "gradu-waited." I went to Western Carolina and your Dad went to study mortuary science. We'd see each other around town over holidays and in the summer. Church socials, that kind of thing. Then I was twenty-two and tired of waiting. So, I asked him out. Told him I'd treat and I'd pick the place.

BRENDA

Where'd you take him?

LILY

The morgue over in Asheville.

BRENDA

Mom, how gross!

LILY

Arranged for a full tour. At first your father thought I was mocking him. But I said now there'd be nothing to shock me about his family business. He was impressed. Impressed enough that you're here to face the same problem. And you will. At least this boy's not as shy as your father. Well, I'd better get you to school.

LILY stands up

                         LILY (cont'd)

You ready?

                         BRENDA

In a minute, Mom.

LILY starts to exit

                         BRENDA (cont'd)

Mom?

                         LILY

Yes?

                         BRENDA

Thanks.

BRENDA goes to LILY and gives her a hug.

BLACK OUT

Scene 13

McAdams Funeral Home - Chapel

Lights up

ACE is seated on one of the chairs by altar. He is thinking. HORACE enters. He is carrying the box with the plaque in it.

                         HORACE

Son.

                         ACE

What?

                         HORACE

You'll be going to church with us Sunday, won't you?

                         ACE

Yes.

                         HORACE

And Christmas Eve service?

ACE

Of course, Dad. I'm not disowning the family.

HORACE

When we're at church Sunday and on Christmas Eve, I want you to look around. How many black faces do you expect to see?

ACE

How many black faces?

HORACE

Yeah . . . How many?

ACE

None.

HORACE

Right. None. And is that my fault?

ACE

Your fault?

HORACE

Yes, my fault. You just accused me of being a racist who has a sign out front reading "Dead Whites Only." Well, look at the heart of this community, the churches, and I'll show you the most segregated hour in the week. If worship divides us into black and white, what do you expect for a funeral? Is that my fault?

ACE

Maybe.

HORACE

Maybe?

JOHN AGEE starts to enter chapel, hears the tone of argument and disappears into the shadows where he can overhear ACE and HORACE. JOHN is not in narrator wardrobe, but is attired to be part of the scene.

ACE

Dad, I'm saying you . . . all of us haven't made the effort to make them feel welcome.

HORACE

That's not true. Your great grandfather even transported a black man once.

ACE

Only because he rode in the back of the hearse.

HORACE

Ace! Would you shut up and listen. It's easy to criticize where we are when you don't know where we've been.

ACE

Okay, Dad. Where have we been that justifies having black churches and white churches worshipping the same God?

HORACE

I'll tell you the justification. Folks like Miss Hattie and Ernie didn't have much else. Their God and their soul. The black church and the black funeral home were the pillars of the black community. Your great grandfather knew that; and when old Mr. Griffin . . . the black man who founded Griffins over in Buncombe County . . . when he came to ask for transport, it was after the other white funeral homes refused to help him.

ACE

You mean the others wanted the business for themselves?

HORACE

No. They told Mr. Griffin they didn't want any "nigger business" that might offend white families. Mr. Griffin only had wagons and horses; he needed a motorized hearse to take the deceased to Georgia. Your great grandfather said grief doesn't know no color and he would get that body back to the family.

ACE

What happened?

HORACE

Mr. Griffin, your great grandfather Horace Sr, and your grandfather, who was only about ten at the time, made the trip the next day. Eight hours it took them. Great granddaddy wouldn't eat in restaurants because Mr. Griffin couldn't get served. They stopped in South Carolina to have lunch at the home of a black family. My dad said he'd never forget it. The table was set inside with just two places: Horace Sr. and his son. Everyone else, including Mr. Griffin, waited for them to eat first.

ACE

See, that's what I'm talking about. When you get left-overs, you expect left-overs.

HORACE

No. We're talking about honor.

ACE

Honor?

HORACE

Yes. Your great grandfather had done a kindness, without expectations or demands. That family was repaying him in the only way they could.

ACE

Right . . .

HORACE

They were honoring him.

ACE

And he still made them wait.

HORACE

He asked once if everyone would join him, and when they said no, he honored their honor by eating the meal. To do otherwise would have been rude.

ACE

And for God's sake, don't be rude. Keep everybody bound in their place with chains of politeness. Don't challenge the way things are. That's Southern hospitality.

HORACE

Knock off the dramatics, Ace. Your great grandfather met them where their need was greatest. Give him credit for that.

ACE

I'll give him that. I'll give him everything. Him and grandpa and you. Just take it all.

HORACE

What do you mean?

ACE

I mean I'm not coming back.

HORACE is too stunned to speak. ACE lets the silence hang for a few seconds, regretting the words.

ACE (cont'd)

Not coming back here to work. I was going to tell you after Christmas. It's not for me. The way we do business. It's dying, Dad.

HORACE

Dying? Of course, it's dying. That is our business.

ACE

It's your business, not mine.

HORACE

It's our family's.

ACE

Dad, I've met a girl.

HORACE

A girl? Who?

ACE

She's in school with me. Maria Rodriguez.

HORACE

Rod . . . Rod . . . Rodriguez?

ACE

Yeah. Rodriguez. As in Senorita. Is that a problem?

HORACE holds his tongue for a beat. Then he tries to be conciliatory.

HORACE

Look, Ace, when we were talking yesterday . . . about women in the business . . . I was just surprised by the thought of your sister. I know times change, and if you and this girl

ACE

Maria. Her name's Maria.

HORACE

If you and Maria are serious and should choose to get married, then she has my blessing to become a working member of the family. Hey, you should have brought her . . . she may be impressed to think she could start her career here.

ACE

Her father owns twenty-five funeral homes across Texas.

HORACE

Twenty-five? Does he bury every Mexican in the state?

ACE

See, Dad. You can't think beyond a white funeral home, a black funeral home, a Mexican funeral home.

HORACE

Well, over in Henderson County they have a Democrat funeral home and a Republican funeral home.

ACE

And what's your point? That you don't care if they're an elephant or a jackass? Maria's father has twenty-five funeral homes because he understands the "business" in the funeral business. And he's offered me a job when I graduate. They're branching out into suburban funeral service centers with all sorts of pre-payment plans.

HORACE

Sort of like HMOs, huh? Why don't they merge together, then they can kill 'em and bury 'em all in one stop.

ACE

Dad, it's a terrific opportunity.

HORACE

And what's this place? A road-side watermelon stand?

HORACE looks down at the package containing the plaque. He slams it down on the altar.

HORACE (cont'd)

Well, thanks for telling me before Christmas. You saved me from making a damn fool of myself. Excuse me. I've got work to do.

HORACE leaves in a huff. ACE stares at the box, starts toward it, then turns and exits in opposite direction from HORACE.

Narrator JOHN AGEE steps from the off-stage shadows. Now he is dressed in narrator outfit and carrying fishing pole. He walks to front of chapel set, closer to audience.

JOHN AGEE

So, I heard it all. Ace tellin' his dad that he didn't want no part of the family bidness. . . . For a place that's supposed to be calm and orderly, McAdams Funeral Home was turnin' into a three-ring circus: Lily strugglin' with Birdie Campbell's eulogy, Ace wrestlin' with guilt over Ernie Roberts, and Horace facin' the end of the McAdams Funeral Home. I felt sorry for him, and after he went and got that plaque and everything. I reckoned I had to do somethin'. I knew Horace Sr. and Horace Jr. were spinnin' like tops in their graves. I just had to figure out what to do.

Well, y'all been good to stay put so long, 'specially you gents with long legs and you women wearin' shoes too tight just because they match your pocketbooks. Why don't y'all stretch a spell. I've got a few things I'm finishin' up myself. Meet ya back here in about fifteen minutes.

JOHN AGEE steps out of the light

BLACK OUT

END OF ACT ONE

ACT TWO

TUESDAY AFTERNOON

Scene 1

McAdams Funeral Home - Chapel

Curtain rises on chapel set lit with single spot light on altar. Boxed plaque is gone. Narrator JOHN AGEE, still dressed in narrator wardrobe steps into beam.

JOHN AGEE

Sorry if I'm late. Time's gettin' away from me now. Where was I? Oh, yeah. I was determined to keep the McAdams Funeral bidness from dyin'. But, I didn't know what to do, other than keep my eyes open for my opportunity.

LIGHTS FADE UP on next scene. LIGHTS FADE OUT on JOHN AGEE.

JOHN

Meanwhile, Tuesday mornin' aged into Tuesday afternoon, and Hattie Roberts and her great niece Tonia arrived to meet Ace.

Scene 2

McAdams Funeral Home - Kitchen

HATTIE ROBERTS, elderly black woman wearing "Sunday-go-to-meetin'" dress and hat and white gloves comes into the kitchen. She is immediately followed by TONIA ROBERTS who wears business attire rather than older-fashion church clothes. ACE comes behind both of them. He is wearing dress shirt, tie, and sports coat.

ACE

Are you sure you don't want to meet in the office, Miss Roberts? It's more comfortable.

HATTIE

There's nothing more comfortable at times like this than a kitchen. All the big decisions in life are kitchen table decisions.

ACE

Then can I get you something? Water? A soft drink?

HATTIE

No, I'm fine.

HATTIE looks around approvingly.

HATTIE (cont'd)

Lot of meals been prepared in here.

TONIA

I don't know why we couldn't have done this at home in our kitchen. We've got family coming in.

ACE

I know this is an inconvenience. I'm sorry. I wanted to meet here so your aunt could see what we have . . . how her brother could be cared for.

TONIA

Cared for? If you'd cared for him proper, we wouldn't be here now. You left him in the car . . . to die.

HATTIE

Tonia. Don't talk like that.

TONIA

It's true, Aunt Hattie. We don't want your care, Mr. McAdams. We've got Griffins and they'll treat us right.

HATTIE

Tonia. You are not speaking for me, and you are not speaking for my brother. I'm sorry, Mr. McAdams. We would be pleased to listen to what you have to say.

ACE

Thank you, ma'am. Believe me, I know how much a funeral costs these days, and I . . . or we wanted to know if you'd accept our services . . . the ones we control . . . for no charge. The casket and vault I can get for you at our cost and there would be a few incidentals . . .

TONIA

Incidentals? I'd think if you feel that guilty, you could throw in a few incidentals.

HATTIE

Hush, child. Nobody has to do anything for guilt. Particularly Mr. McAdams. His family's already helped us once.

TONIA/ACE

They/We have?

HATTIE

When my grandfather Willie died, Mr. Horace Sr. carried him back to Georgia where he was born. Our family didn't have no other way to get him there, and Mr. Horace wouldn't accept one penny.

ACE

He had a good meal in South Carolina.

HATTIE

That's what my momma said. So, y'all haven't forgotten. I'm sad to say Tonia doesn't seem to know our family history so well.

TONIA

I know Granddaddy's history in Birmingham.

HATTIE

Umm. Don't let God's blossom of kindness be overgrown by the Devil's weeds, child.

ACE

It was an honor for my great grandfather to serve your family, Miss Roberts. I would like to have the same opportunity.

HATTIE

I don't know. This is a nice place, but it isn't our place. Ernie's been gone from here a long time. The connections with our people are stronger at Griffins. I don't mean to insult your kindness.

HATTIE suddenly stands up. ACE and TONIA do likewise.

HATTIE (cont'd)

No. Keep your seats. Both of you. I need to pray on this a few moments. I'm going to the chapel. I know the way. Tonia, I want you and Mr. McAdams . . .

ACE

Ace, please.

HATTIE

I want you and Ace to talk to each other . . . about this . . . about anything. Because whatever we decide, we're going to leave here as friends. I'll be back shortly.

HATTIE exits.

ACE

Well, Tonia, I guess we got our orders.

TONIA

You mean I got my orders. You're already doing what she wants.

ACE

I'm just trying to do what's right.

TONIA

And I'm not?

ACE doesn't answer. Silence hangs a few seconds.

TONIA (cont'd)

My grandfather doesn't need you to honor him.

ACE

No, he doesn't, but I know from talking with him that he would have been kind enough to let me . . . like my great grandfather was kind enough to eat your family's meal with everybody watching him.

TONIA

Oh, yes. This meal in South Carolina. And your great grandfather, the one I'm neglecting to admire. Guess that was a big deal. Passed down from generation to generation. "That time we helped the colored folks."

ACE

I learned about it this morning.

TONIA

This morning? But you told my aunt . . .

ACE

I told your aunt my great grandfather had a good meal in South Carolina. My father told me the story this morning because I called him a racist.

TONIA

Is he?

ACE

He didn't want to handle your grandfather's funeral. I thought it was because he was black and we're a white funeral home. But I was wrong. The problem's not that your grandfather's black; it's that you're black and as much a racist as my father.

TONIA is furious. She leans in toward ACE.

TONIA

What?!

ACE

Well, how would you feel if you were told don't help . . . you're not the right color?

TONIA

Oh, but I have been told that . . . to my face.

ACE

And did you give up?

TONIA

What do you think?

ACE

Then why should I give up trying to do the right thing just because I'm not the right color?

TONIA thinks about his words for a few seconds.

TONIA

It's not that you're not appreciated.

ACE

You have a strange way of showing it.

TONIA again considers what ACE said. After a few seconds, grief overcomes anger.

TONIA

It's just that . . .

She pauses, struggling through emotions to reach the words.

ACE

What?

TONIA

It's just that he was my grandfather, and I loved him very much. . . . I'm not sure what to do. Hattie doesn't understand the world is changing. She won't listen. She thinks I don't know anything.

ACE

Yeah, Dad's the same way. And John . . . John Agee actually worked with my great grandfather. Don't get him started on the way things used to be. Old folks. Whatcha going to do with them?

TONIA

Take care of them. Protect Aunt Hattie. That's all I'm trying to do.

ACE

Protect her from what? White people? Protect her from me?

TONIA

From the past. You don't know where she's been.

ACE

No, I don't. I wasn't there. But I'm here. In this moment. Maybe I'm bringing baggage; maybe you're bringing baggage; but it's the only moment for us right now. I'd like to use it to help.

TONIA

Then leave us alone. We're better off doing things our own way. That's not racism; that's reality.

ACE

Oh, I get it. Some people find racism as reality only when it's convenient.

TONIA

That's right. It's convenient for you to call me a racist because the reality is you left my grandfather in that car.

TONIA turns her back on ACE.

BLACK OUT

Scene 3

McAdams Funeral Home - Chapel

(Lights up. HATTIE enters the chapel. LILY is watering flowers set out on the altar. LILY turns as she hears footsteps.)

LILY

Oh, Miss Hattie. I'm so sorry about your brother. I'm Lily McAdams. Please accept our condolences.

HATTIE

I remember you. You've been very kind. Your son and my great niece are going over some things in the kitchen. I thought I'd come in here for awhile, if that's all right.

LILY

Yes. I often do that too. That's why I like flowers in here even when there's no service. There are quiet moments I like to take by myself. You just stay as long as you want.

HATTIE

Thank you.

LILY

Miss Hattie. I know this might not be the time, but Ace told me your brother was coming back for Birdie Campbell's funeral. And you sent flowers. I'd like to say something nice tomorrow . . . about Birdie. I hate to think that she or anyone would go through a memorial service here without a memory . . . a story . . . that reflects upon her life in a way . . . in a way that shows she made a difference.

HATTIE

And what do you have for Birdie?

LILY

Nothing, really. Some greeting card sentiments copied out of a poetry book. That - and a few quotes handed to me on bouquets sent as obligations.

HATTIE

I'm sorry, Lily. Sorry there's not more I can tell you. Ernie, Birdie, and I knew each other as little kids. My mother worked for hers, and we played together until we went our separate ways in separate schools. When you reach my age and someone from your childhood passes over, it's a part of your life too.

LILY

You mean your brother rode all night to be at the funeral for a woman who hadn't been a friend since you were little kids?

HATTIE

Like I said – you get my age those times become more precious.

LILY

Yes, but that says more about the character of you and your brother than it does about Birdie. I'm not sure she deserved such friends.

HATTIE is silent. She closes her eyes as if praying.

LILY (cont'd)

Miss Hattie? Can I bring you something? Water? Co-cola?

HATTIE

No, I'm fine. You don't know if Mr. Agee's about, do you?

LILY

John?

HATTIE

We knew each other a long time ago.

LILY

He's here somewhere. Last I saw him he was repairing the bottom of the lectern. He's afraid I'll lean on it and topple over. I can get him for you.

HATTIE

No, don't bother. I just thought he might be near.

LILY

If I see him, I'll tell him you're here. Now, Miss Hattie, you stay as long as you want.

LILY exits.

HATTIE sits down and bows her head in prayer.

BLACK OUT

Scene 4

McAdams Funeral Home - Kitchen

ACE is sitting at the kitchen table. TONIA is still standing, as if looking out a window in direction of audience. SILENCE for a few seconds. TONIA glances at her watch.

TONIA

I wonder what's taking Aunt Hattie so long?

ACE

She's giving our offer consideration. What if she accepts? Are you going to argue with her?

TONIA answers without facing him.

                    TONIA

No. If you promise not to argue if she declines.

                    ACE

All right. But, whatever she decides, I can still make the calls to the hospital and to Griffins.

TONIA smiles to herself, thinking how ACE is determined to help somehow. She turns around and walks over to sit in the chair.

                    TONIA

How about the minister?

                    ACE

You should call him. He'll want to meet with you.

                    TONIA

Okay.

                    ACE

The college needs to know. I can take care of that. And your grandfather's band.

                    TONIA

You ever hear them play?

                    ACE

No. He told me about them on the ride up here. Said they'd cut a track for a CD - "Sounds of Bourbon Street."

                    TONIA

One of those collections - preserving the authentic music before it dies out. . . . (She pauses, reflecting on the words). Dies out. A lot died out with granddaddy. I wish you could have heard him play his horn.

                    ACE

I do too. Missie T.

                    TONIA

He told you my special name? Did he talk about me?

ACE

Oh, yeah. He was proud of you all right.

ACE gets up and walks to kitchen counter. He picks up a brown shopping bag.

ACE (cont'd)

He put his suitcase and this paper bag in my trunk. There's a Christmas present for "Sis" and one for "My Missie T."

ACE hands her a wrapped CD. TONIA takes the gift, looks at the tag, and rubs her hand over the writing as if able to touch her grandfather. Her grief starts to break through.

TONIA

"Missie T." When I was a teenager, I was embarrassed when he called me that. Now, I'd give anything . . .

TONIA chokes up. ACE sits down quietly, not interrupting her private thoughts. TONIA looks at the package and blinks back tears.

TONIA (cont'd)

I know what it is . . . The CD - "Sounds of Bourbon Street." Did he tell you what song the record company chose?

ACE hesitates . . . then nods his head.

TONIA (cont'd)

What?

ACE

Just A Closer Walk With Thee.

TONIA shakes her head at the irony.

TONIA

The classic New Orleans funeral dirge. And here we are . . . in a funeral home.

ACE and TONIA sit in silence for a few seconds.

ACE

Tonia . . . I wish I'd invited him in.

TONIA doesn't answer, just stares at him.

ACE (cont'd)

I thought he was sleeping. I was glad he was sleeping.

TONIA

(without sarcasm)

You were only running in for a few moments.

ACE

And I was glad he was sleeping because he had made me feel guilty.

TONIA

Guilty?

ACE

He didn't want my folks to worry and insisted I stop in before taking him home.

TONIA

That sounds like Granddaddy. Why the guilt?

ACE

Because he was so excited about seeing you and his sister, and being back in these mountains. And I didn't want to come home.

TONIA

You didn't?

ACE

Oh, I wanted to see Mom and Dad and my sister for Christmas. Sure. But . . . well, it's not important. You don't need to hear this.

TONIA

Aren't you the next son in McAdams and Son?

ACE

I want to live my own life. Not some script written for me.

TONIA

What are you going to do? Drop out?

ACE

No. I've got a job offer in Texas.

TONIA

Texas? To bury people?

ACE

Yes.

TONIA

Why Texas?

ACE

It's a big corporation. And the father of one of my classmates owns it.

TONIA

So, you and he will work together?

ACE

Well, she's a girl.

TONIA

As in girlfriend?

ACE

It's a good business opportunity.

TONIA

Girlfriend. Well, I hope it works out. Sometimes working together can be tough.

ACE

You saying that from experience?

TONIA

Nothing that broke my heart. I dated a guy I worked with in social services.

ACE

Job get in the way?

TONIA

He got in the way. Robert was white. Didn't take me long to realize he went out with me so he could show me off. I was a black trophy, and he was proving something to his family and friends. He kept telling me how liberal he was. I decided I couldn't bring that jerk home to Aunt Hattie, especially since I know she wouldn't want me crossing the color line.

ACE

Really?

TONIA

She's old school, and Robert wasn't worth upsetting her.

ACE

But someone else might be?

TONIA

What do you mean?

ACE

I don't know. Just wondering if you'd made a rule.

TONIA

A rule? Like "I shalt not date white guys." No white guys; no white funeral homes. And the ultimate "no-no" -- a white guy in a white funeral home. Good thing you've got that Texas business opportunity.

ACE

(half-heartedly)

Yeah, good thing.

TONIA

Well, why don't you show me around? Aunt Hattie will find us when she's ready.

TONIA and ACE exit.

HORAC enters and starts pulling together bread, peanut butter and jelly for a sandwich.

LILY enters.

LILY

Here you are.

HORACE

Here I am.

LILY

I could have fixed you more for lunch if you're still hungry.

HORACE

I may not be a great businessman, but I am capable of making a peanut butter and jelly sandwich.

LILY

Businessman? What's wrong, Horace?

HORACE

Nothing. Everything is just terrific. Everything is just . . . just Bueno. Muy bueno.

LILY

Bueno?

HORACE

Oh, yeah. Unbelievably bueno. . . . Lily, how many Mexicans do you think live in the mountains?

LILY

Mexicans?

HORACE

Well, maybe not Mexico Mexicans. But your Spanish types.

LILY

I don't know. A few hundred? If you're counting a couple counties? Maybe more in the summer when some Cuban-Americans are up from Florida.

HORACE

Are you including Asheville?

LILY

Horace. What's this about?

HORACE

There's bound to be more than a hundred, counting Asheville. Lily, I'm talking about expanding. Looking for an opportunity. Bilingual funerals.

LILY

Us? Bilingual? Horace, you couldn't understand that old man from Boston who was asking you where to "pahk his cah."

HORACE

We would hire someone. Someone who speaks Spanish. Someone just starting in the business. Maybe get some investors to open a Spanish funeral home. "McAdams Casa de Muerte."

LILY

Casa de Muerte? Horace, that means House of Death.

HORACE

Well, I couldn't find funeral in Brenda's Berlitz Phrase Book. But you get the point.

LILY

No, I don't get the point. This sounds like something Ace would think up. Not you.

HORACE

The world is changing, Lily. Even Ridgetop. I've got to think of Ace's future too.

LILY

Horace. Look. I just left Miss Hattie praying in the chapel. She doesn't know whether to let us handle her brother's funeral, and we've known her for years. Do you really think strangers with a strange language are going to feel any different? This is about Ace, isn't it? Ace and Maria?

HORACE

You knew about Maria?

LILY

I'm a mother. It's my job to know about my son's girlfriends.

HORACE

Did he tell you about the job? About working for her father?

LILY

No. But I'm not surprised. Like you said, the world is changing. And it's a big, wide-open world for Ace. I also wouldn't be surprised if it all blows over. Maria's his third girlfriend in the last year.

HORACE

I wish you'd told me about her.

LILY

So you could just worry? Make yourself sandwiches you don't need to eat? He's gonna find his own way, Horace. The more you try to hold him down, the more he's gonna struggle to break loose. I hope you haven't mentioned this casa de muerte to him.

HORACE

No.

LILY

Good. Don't.

HORACE

You don't think he'll leave, do you, Lily?

LILY

I don't know. It is his future. But if you push him, Horace, it won't be his leaving that'll be the problem. It'll be his ever coming back. You could lose more than a partner.

HORACE

But being a McAdams son is being a partner, Lily. That's the way it's always been.

LILY

Then I don't know what to tell you. Except I'm not getting in the middle between two people I love. I'm afraid you're on your own.

BLACK OUT

Scene 5

McAdams Funeral Home - Chapel

Lights up on HATTIE, sitting and praying silently. JOHN AGEE enters in his work clothes, carrying a simple lectern. He quietly sets it down beside the altar. HATTIE opens her eyes, looks at him and remains silent.

As they speak their opening lines, there is a hint of unspoken tension.

JOHN

Hello, Hattie.

HATTIE

John.

Pause of awkward silence as JOHN searches for way to begin.

JOHN

I'm real sorry about Ernie.

HATTIE

Everybody else seems to be too, John.

JOHN

I ain't ever-body else.

HATTIE

No. No, you're not.

JOHN

Hattie, where did they go?

HATTIE

I left them in the kitchen.

JOHN

The years, Hattie. I meant the years. Where did the years go?

HATTIE

Oh, you know. They just . . . go.

JOHN

I rode up to Stony Pond last night. Thinkin' about Ernie. Rememberin' us. Now there's a gate across the road and a guardhouse. I couldn't get to the flat rock.

HATTIE

Ernie's favorite fishin' spot.

JOHN

Our spot too, Hattie. Seems like only yesterday. Now it's a "planned community." Stony Pond Estates. Estates. Condos of rich retirees who fish dressed out of a catalogue.

HATTIE

Ernie was right, John. It was not meant to be. You and me. Not back in those times.

JOHN

I was young and foolish. (He steps back a pace and chuckles.) But Ernie tried to knock some sense in my head . . . my jaw too. Still, I shoulda been there for ya in other times . . . in other ways. I've tried to keep my eye on ya. In my own way.

HATTIE

I know, John. Would you do me a favor now?

JOHN

Name it.

HATTIE

Young Ace and my great niece Tonia are working out what to do about Ernie's funeral arrangements. He's a nice young man. I see a lot of Horace Sr. in him.

JOHN

I would have hoped so.

HATTIE

I want you to be the one to take care of Ernie's body. He was coming back for Birdie's funeral, but he wanted to see you again.

JOHN

You talked?

HATTIE

Yes, on the phone. I called with the news about Birdie. Ernie said it may be getting time to come home for good. He was right. He was always right.

JOHN

Maybe that's one good thing about Birdie's dyin' when she did.

HATTIE

Yes . . . Birdie.

JOHN

She used to be fun, when we were kids. What happened to her?

HATTIE

It's what didn't happen to her. You remember Arlo Justus.

JOHN

That in'surance man? He's been gone for must be forty years.

HATTIE

He was supposed to marry Birdie, but he left her for a waitress in Asheville. She never let anyone get close to her again.

JOHN

Hattie, I'm sorry if I hurt ya.

HATTIE

You didn't hurt me, John. You and I didn't have a choice. That guardhouse was up at Stony Pond years ago for you and me.

HATTIE looks at the card on one of Birdie's bouquets

HATTIE (cont'd)

Poor Birdie. Mrs. McAdams said she hates there's no story . . . no memory showing Birdie made a difference. That's weighing on my soul, John.

JOHN

You have a story, don't you? You and Ernie?

HATTIE

It was just between us. I promised her that.

JOHN

She told me, Hattie. Right after . . . right after it happened. She knew we'd been close once. I guess I was hurt you couldn't come to me. But what's done is done. And what's said is said. I don't think there's a promise to keep now. Not to Birdie.

HATTIE

Maybe. Maybe not.

JOHN

I'd be honored to take care of Ernie wherever you decide. Now, I need something from you.

HATTIE

What?

JOHN

Some words . . . somehow . . . to Ace. He's plannin' on leavin'.

HATTIE

Leaving?

JOHN

He told his dad the ways of this place are old-fashioned. He wants to join some big chain in Texas. And there's a girl.

HATTIE

There's always a girl . . . or a boy.

HATTIE looks around the chapel, then back at JOHN.

HATTIE (cont'd)

Old fashioned? Including you?

JOHN

I reckon. Young folks. Whatcha gonna do with 'em?

HATTIE

My Tonia's twenty-five and knows it all. The old stories are just that . . . old stories. I might as well be straight off the plantation. Can't talk sense to my own niece. How am I suppose to talk to Ace?

JOHN

I thought maybe, since he's feelin' guilty about Ernie, maybe you could get through to him. His father's got the gift of saying the wrong thing at just the right time. And Ace won't listen to me.

HATTIE

Why not?

JOHN

Cause I'm just an old mountain coot. Been here so long I'm part of the furniture. But if you tell him how comfortin' it is . . . to have someone who grew up in the town . . . you know, it might get him thinkin'.

HATTIE

How many seventy-five-year-old women did you listen to when you were his age?

JOHN

None, but then I wasn't buryin' their brother.

HATTIE

All right. We'll see.

HATTIE stands up.

JOHN

Thank you, Hattie.

There is a beat of silence, then they hug each other close, swaying together as if both are hearing some slow sad song.

TONIA and ACE enter without HATTIE and JOHN seeing them.

HATTIE and JOHN step apart a few inches. JOHN tenderly caresses her cheek.

TONIA is shocked and speechless. She stands stunned for a few seconds, then runs away. ACE follows her.

BLACK OUT

Scene 6

McAdams Funeral Home - Kitchen

LIGHTS FADE UP

TONIA enters. She is visibly upset. ACE follows.

                    ACE

I don't think they saw us.

                    TONIA

Don't talk about it. I don't want to talk about it.

                    ACE

Okay.

TONIA waits a few agitated beats, and then can't contain herself.

                    TONIA

Well, who was that?

                    ACE

John. John Agee. He works here.

                    TONIA

He works here? My grandfather's just died and your employee puts moves on my great aunt?

                    ACE

Moves? From John? A turtle has faster moves. If there was any moving going on, it looked mutual to me.

TONIA

I said I don't want to talk about it.

ACE

Okay. I forgot. You must be old school . . . old rule.

TONIA

What's that supposed to mean?

ACE

A white guy in a white funeral home. So, you've extended your rule to your aunt and a seventy-six-year-old mountaineer.

TONIA

That's different. Aunt Hattie's . . . vulnerable. She's a victim.

ACE

A victim? Of John Agee? Believe me, John Agee is not one to parade a woman around as a trophy -- black or white. I think the reality here is you don't like what you saw. You can cross the color line but your aunt's not allowed. Now explain the difference between racism and reality again.

TONIA angrily turns away.

TONIA

I said I don't want to talk about it.

ACE

Well, I'm glad we're not talking about it because I don't know what to say.

TONIA

If you don't know what to say, then do us both a big favor and keep quiet.

ACE

Sometimes keeping quiet is easier said than done. (He thinks about what he said.) That's funny. "Keeping quiet is easier said than done." If you've said it, you're not keeping quiet.

TONIA

Are you always this weird?

ACE

Except it's true. Just because you don't know what to say doesn't mean you can keep quiet. That's my mother's problem.

TONIA

She can't keep quiet either? Must run in the family.

ACE

She has to say something about Birdie Campbell. At the funeral tomorrow.

TONIA

Your mother doesn't like to speak in public?

ACE

She doesn't like to lie in public. Birdie didn't exactly leave a memorable trail of good deeds.

TONIA

Aunt Hattie sent flowers.

ACE

You said you didn't know they were friends.

TONIA

Aunt Hattie never mentioned her before.

ACE

Did you ask her why she was sending flowers?

TONIA

Yes. She said she didn't want to talk about it.

ACE

She didn't want to talk about it. You don't want to talk about it. Must run in the family.

TONIA

If your mother can't keep quiet, what's she going to say about Birdie Campbell?

ACE

Your guess is as good as mine. Better probably.

TONIA turns around to face ACE.

> TONIA

Why's that?

> ACE

Birdie must have been close to your whole family. Your grandfather told me he was coming back for the funeral.

> TONIA

Birdie Campbell's? Did he say why?

> ACE

No, not really. He said he'd known Birdie a long time ago. He was obliged -- that's the word he used . . . "obliged" -- he was obliged to her. I laughed and said I never heard of anyone obliged to Birdie Campbell. How'd he let that happen?

> TONIA

What'd he say?

> ACE

He said he couldn't talk about it.

> TONIA

Couldn't or wouldn't?

> ACE

Couldn't. Then he told me to remember everybody is two people: the outside that we show each other and the inside that God sees. For some people, they are close to the same. For others, the inside person only comes out in special moments -- for good or evil. Your grandfather said he was coming back for the inside Birdie -- the one who had gone to God.

> TONIA

And that was it?

> ACE

Then he was quiet. I thought . . . I thought he was sleeping.

> TONIA

But he was gone to God.

TONIA turns away again, not because she is angry, but because she doesn't want ACE to see her crying.

HATTIE enters, followed by JOHN AGEE.

HATTIE

I'm sorry to have left you so long. Tonia, did you and Ace make any decisions?

TONIA turns around and looks past her aunt to JOHN.

TONIA

(slightly accusatory tone)

Who's he?

JOHN

I'm John Agee. I work here.

TONIA

You work here. So, what's your opinion, Mr. Agee?

JOHN

Opinion of what?

TONIA

Of what we should do.

JOHN

It's no opinion, young lady. It's a statement. We should do what makes Hattie . . .Miss Roberts. . . the most comfortable.

TONIA nods in agreement and looks back and forth between JOHN and HATTIE trying to puzzle out the relationship.

TONIA

Aunt Hattie, you said our connections were stronger at Griffins.

HATTIE

Yes, I did. (She looks at John, then back at her niece.) But we are part of this community as well. What do you think, Ace?

TONIA

He agreed not to argue against your wishes.

HATTIE

I wish to hear his opinion. His honest opinion.

ACE

This is just an opinion. (He glances at TONIA who is staring him down.) We are happy to do everything we can, but I think you would be more comfortable if you held the service at Griffins.

HATTIE

You do?

TONIA

He does.

HATTIE

Then I agree.

JOHN

But . . .

ACE

But I think the arrangements with the hospital, the embalming procedure, and the transportation to Griffins should be handled by us at no charge.

HATTIE

You do?

JOHN

He does.

HATTIE

Then I agree. Will John . . .Mr. Agee be helping?

ACE looks behind HATTIE at JOHN, not sure of the reason for her question. JOHN nods his head.

ACE

Yes, if that's all right?

HATTIE (cont'd)

Mr. Agee and my brother were fishing buddies. I think it's more than all right. It's what Ernie wants. You are a blessing, Ace.

ACE

We're glad to be of service.

HATTIE

I can't give you lunch in South Carolina, but I'll have you by the house. You don't know what a comfort it is to entrust my brother to someone who's grown up here. You and Mr. Agee are not strangers . . . to me . . . (Hattie gives a pointed look at Tonia.) . . . nor to my family. That means a lot at times like this. Like Tonia always tells me, those in need don't care what color the hands are that help them. . . Now, we'd best be on our way.

HATTIE gives a goodbye nod to each man. TONIA nods to ACE, then looks warily at JOHN, still suspecting something.

ACE

I'll walk you to your car.

ACE, TONIA, and HATTIE exit. JOHN watches them leave. A slight smile breaks across his face.

BLACK OUT

Scene 7

McAdams Funeral Home - Kitchen

Lights up

Telephone is ringing. LILY McADAMS comes in and answers it.

LILY

McAdams Funeral Directors, Lily speaking . . . Oh, good afternoon, Mrs. Dickerson. (listens) Things couldn't be going smoother. Don't you worry. Everything will be ready for your sister's funeral tomorrow. You and your son are still driving up in the morning, aren't you? (listens) Yes, if you leave at eight, you should be fine. (listens) Yes, I'll be making a few remarks. (listens) Well, it's hard to know where to begin. There's so much I could say about Birdie. So, I think it will be better to keep it short. I don't want to slight anybody who told me wonderful stories. Say, do you have something in particular you'd want me to remember about Birdie? (listens) Oh, I didn't realize you were a lot younger. (listens) You ran away at sixteen?. . Yes, I understand how older sisters can be bossy. . . Yes, if someone's always giving you a piece of their mind, you could lose your own. So, you and Birdie weren't close? (listens) That long since you've seen her? (listens) No, I'm sure you'll recognize her. She'll be the one in the casket. Yes, Mrs. Dickerson. We're right off Main Street. Goodbye. (hangs up) Damn! This funeral's gonna kill me.

BLACK OUT

Scene 8

McAdams Funeral Home - Chapel, later Tuesday

Lights up

ACE is standing behind the lectern, running his hands across the surface. He looks at the altar and then around the room, thinking.

JOHN AGEE enters in his work clothes.

JOHN

I remember when you use to sneak in here and stand up on a chair behind this lectern.

ACE

Pretending to be a preacher.

JOHN

And every time your dad caught you, me and your grandpa would come to your defense.

ACE

Long time ago.

JOHN

Only yesterday to me. You'll see how the years fly by. Ace, ya done good workin' out Ernie's funeral arrangements.

ACE

I suspect you and Miss Hattie had already made that decision.

JOHN

I've known Miss Hattie a long time, Ace. What do ya think of her?

ACE

I like her. She's open-minded and wants to do the right thing. I think she was teaching a lesson.

JOHN

What did ya learn?

ACE

Me? She was teaching a lesson to Tonia. Miss Hattie made her face that everything isn't black and white.

JOHN

You didn't learn anything?

ACE

Well, I guess I was too hard on Dad, calling this place a lily white funeral home. He was right. They are more comfortable at Griffins.

JOHN

That's it? What about being part of the community? Hattie wantin' to turn her brother over to someone who knew him?

ACE

That was you, John. I'm just doing my job helping you.

JOHN

Well, you're wrong. I just can't believe how wrong.

ACE

What are you talking about?

JOHN

I overheard you tellin' your dad about that Texas job, that's what.

ACE

You agree with Dad?

JOHN

Of course not. He's wrong too. But then he usually is.

ACE

So, I'm wrong to go and wrong to stay. Great.

JOHN

No. You're wrong to go. And you're wrong to stay because your dad says he needs ya. You should stay because the people of this community need ya. People like Hattie and her niece.

ACE

But the big chains are the wave of the future.

JOHN

Didn't ya learn nothin' in that college besides embalmin'? There's no future to the funeral bidness. It's the past ... the memory of the past. And that ain't changed since the Pharaohs built them pyramids. I may be 76, hell nearly 77, but I wasn't born yesterday. That branch service bidness has as much chance of succeeding in Texas as me turnin' the Alamo into one of them taco stands. People ain't goin' to give a loved one to a stranger just because he has a drive-thru window and takes a credit card.

ACE

John, you don't understand. I'm not needed here. There's you and Dad. And someday they'll be somebody else. Somebody who wants to work here.

JOHN

Somebody else?

JOHN becomes even more agitated. He goes behind the altar and picks up the box with the plaque.

JOHN (cont'd)

This is the Christmas present you saved your dad the embarrassment of givin' you. Well, I ain't gonna spare ya. Look at it! Just look at it!

JOHN pulls out the plaque and shoves it in ACE's hands.

>   JOHN (cont'd)
> Ace, people need ya in this town because you are Horace
> McAdams the Fourth. They look at ya and see the past that's
> Horace McAdams the Third, and Horace McAdams, Jr., and
> Horace McAdams, Sr. You're the bridge to moments that
> happened years ago, but will blaze back for 'em at a time of
> remembrance. You go to Texas . . . you go to Texas and you
> close the door on them and their past.

>   ACE
> John, you're getting too upset.

>   JOHN
> Hell, I ain't upset enough. You . . . you walk out on this town .
> . . you walk out on these people . . . and you'll see upset. Well,
> I ain't gonna watch it. I ain't gonna see this bidness die . . . I
> ain't gonna see you kill it. By God, I . . . I . . . I quit!

JOHN storms off stage. ACE is left holding the plaque. He looks down and silently reads it again.

BLACK OUT

Scene 9

WEDNESDAY MORNING

McAdams Funeral Home - Kitchen

Lights up

LILY is setting out cereal bowls, juice, and milk as in the earlier scenes. HORACE enters and sits down. They do not speak. ACE enters and sits. No one speaks. They begin eating in silence.

Lights up on Narrator JOHN AGEE

JOHN is in narrator wardrobe including hat and fishing pole. He stands in spotlight in chapel area, looking back and forth between audience and kitchen scene.

JOHN

The funeral home was not its usual happy, lively self on Wednesday morning. Guess I was to blame for most of it. I had sure surprised myself, quittin' with five seconds notice after over fifty years. So, I reckon Horace, Ace, and Lily were in shock . . . sorta like bein' in a bad car wreck. Lily still had to get through Birdie Campbell's eulogy; Horace had lost his right arm – me, and he knew he was losin' his son as well; Ace was just broodin' because he had become the center of the storm and didn't know which way to turn. None of 'em wanted to talk cause there was nothin' they could say.

BRENDA enters. She is dressed in a bright Christmas sweater and she is cheery as can be.

JOHN (cont'd)

The only one who didn't act down-in-the-mouth was Brenda. What a difference a day makes.

Light fades out on JOHN.

BRENDA sits down and fixes her cereal.

BRENDA

Good morning.

HORACE, LILY, ACE merely grunt.

BRENDA (cont'd)

I said good morning, family. Where's the Christmas cheer? It's my first day of vacation.

ACE/LILY/HORACE

(subdued)

Good morning.

BRENDA

Well, don't knock yourselves out with jubilation. A simple "bah humbug" will do.

They continue eating. BRENDA breaks silence again.

BRENDA (cont'd)

Mom. I was thinking about making some Christmas cookies this morning.

LILY

Today's not a good day, dear. I need you to help get ready for Birdie's funeral.

BRENDA

Me? Where's John?

LILY

He's gone.

BRENDA

Gone? Gone where?

No one answers immediately. BRENDA looks around the table.

HORACE

He quit.

BRENDA

Quit? John quit?

HORACE

Yes. He quit.

BRENDA

Not John. He's part of the family. You don't quit your family.

HORACE

Some people do.

BRENDA

Why didn't anybody tell me? I'm part of this family too? Ace?

ACE

I was still trying to talk him out of it. I even went to his house last night.

BRENDA

Was he there?

ACE

He wouldn't see me.

BRENDA

What did he say?

ACE

He hollered through the door he was going to bed so he could get up and go fishing.

BRENDA

Fishing? I can't believe he'd walk out on a funeral and go fishing.

HORACE

We're just going to have to pull together until I can find somebody to help.

BRENDA's teenage giddiness has crashed into irrational teenage despair.

BRENDA

But John can't quit. I was going to make cookies. Chris Murphy is coming over to study. Mom, you know how important this is.

LILY

Horace, it's not Brenda's fault John quit. Let's get the chapel ready now. Then she can bake while . . . while I pull something together to say for Birdie. Lord, help us all.

BLACK OUT

Scene 10

McAdams Funeral Home - Empty Stage Left

Fade up single spotlight on Narrator

JOHN AGEE is in narrator wardrobe with fishing pole and cap.

JOHN

Lord, help us all. That pretty much summed up the sorry situation. The McAdams family scrambled to pull off a funeral service without the help of yours truly.

Pre-recorded track of piano hymn "Peace Like A River" rises under JOHN.

JOHN (cont'd)

And I was at home when I realized that in over fifty years, I had never been to a funeral as . . . well . . . as a spectator.

Lights up on Chapel Area.

A few rows of folding chairs have been set up in front of lectern and altar. Kitchen set has been withdrawn so that chapel set is sole set on stage and play audience becomes audience for funeral.

VARIETY OF "TOWNSPEOPLE" are sitting in folding chairs. HORACE, ACE, LILY are on front row. HATTIE and TONIA are on second. A few seats are vacant. Music continues.

PREACHER WINFIELD is at the lectern reading the 23rd Psalm in a voice low enough so that it doesn't overpower JOHN.

JOHN (cont'd)

Just because I quit a funeral home didn't mean I couldn't visit a funeral home. What did I have to be afraid of? Birdie Campbell weren't goin' to run me off. I wouldn't make it at the very start, but that was okay. I didn't want to detract from Birdie's big day and figured I could slip in on the sly. You know . . . while the preacher was readin' somethin' out of the Good Book.

Fade out JOHN's spotlight

PREACHER WINFIELD increases his speaking volume. Mourners may join in.

WINFIELD

Yea, though I walk through the valley of the shadow of death, I will fear no evil: for thou art with me; thy rod and thy staff they comfort me. Thou preparest a table before me in the presence of mine enemies: thou anointest my head with oil; my cup runneth over. Surely goodness and mercy shall follow me all the days of my life; and I will dwell in the house of the Lord for ever. Amen

And Miss Birdie Campbell is dwelling in the house of the Lord. She has come out from under the shadow of death and is standing in the pure light of Almighty God. There is nothing more glorious to be said for her, but there are some things to be said for us . . . and to us, her friends and family. Mrs. Lily McAdams will now remember Birdie Campbell.

LILY is lost in thought. She has to be nudged into realizing it is time to speak. She gets up from her front row seat and walks to the lectern.

PREACHER WINFIELD stands to one side. LILY holds a few sheets of paper in her hand. She looks at the funeral audience and the general audience, then looks at the papers in her hand.

LILY

I had some words prepared . . . flowery words out of books . . . but they weren't my words . . . weren't honest words. Now Birdie Campbell was known by us all. She was a woman who always spoke to everyone she met . . . whether you wanted to hear from her or not. But, she always spoke honestly and I respect that. Birdie was a woman gifted with a mind of her own who took whatever time necessary to share a piece of that mind with others. Birdie had a unique effect on everyone who knew her. People she touched were never quite the same.

JOHN AGEE comes in and slips into a seat near HATTIE and TONIA. EVERYONE notices his entry. His appearance breaks LILY's train of thought for a second.

LILY (cont'd)

. . . And there are people who touch our lives, and we never realize how much until that touch is gone. Well, Birdie has gone from us now . . . but I know somehow the world is a better place . . . for her having been here. I want each of us to take a moment of silence to remember Birdie, and if you have a special story and are so inclined, I invite you to come forward so that we can all share your remembrance.

There is a span of silence for 10-15 seconds. People avoid eye-contact with LILY and each other. Then HATTIE ROBERTS stands. TONIA takes her arm, trying to pull her back to her seat, but HATTIE shakes her off. She takes a few steps to the end of the aisle where JOHN is seated, halts, and takes a deep breath.

JOHN rises and then assists her in walking to the lectern with a "wedding" formality. LILY steps back beside WINFIELD and nods at HATTIE appreciatively. JOHN stands next to HATTIE.

HATTIE

I'm not used to speaking in public and Lord knows it's hard enough to get up here and say words I promised would never cross my lips. But, John, that is, Mr. Agee, . . .

HATTIE smiles and thinks a second.

HATTIE (cont'd)

No, my dear friend John reminded me we are known by our stories . . . moments in our lives that make us who we are. I have such a moment with Birdie, and I know as well as I'm standing in front of y'all that I've no right to keep it a secret . . . now is not the time for a moment of silence.

Y'all may know my brother Ernie passed over last Monday. It happened as he reached home through the kindness of Mr. Horace McAdams the Fourth. But, Ernie was coming home to pay his respects to Birdie, and so I have a double responsibility to him and to Birdie.

HATTIE fumbles in her pocketbook and pulls out a high school graduation picture of a young black man, simply framed, circa 1960.

HATTIE (cont'd)

I brought along in my pocketbook a photograph which has been beside my bed for over 35 years. Ernie's oldest boy, James Roberts - my nephew and the uncle that Tonia never knew. In the early sixties, he worked with Dr. King in Birmingham and Selma. He was the apple of my eye . . . and . . . (HATTIE pauses). . . and he was blown apart when the Klan bombed his church. He and seven little children he was teaching Sunday School. . . gone to God . . . in a moment. Here in Ridgetop, the Gazette wrote it was an "unfortunate incident" ignited by "agitators outside of Alabama." Well, I was outside of Alabama and didn't have any money to get to the funeral.

HATTIE pauses again as the emotions from the past sweep over her. She looks around the chapel and audience.

HATTIE (cont'd)

I know what y'all are thinking. I went to Birdie Campbell and because my mama had worked for her mama, and we knew each other as children, she loaned me money, or maybe even gave me money to get to Alabama. Well, what Birdie gave me was better than money. She picked me up in her Buick car and drove me straight through to Birmingham. Eight hours it took us. She stayed with me at my brother Ernie's house with white cops on every corner, just a glarin' at her when she went by, and her a glarin' right back like we all know she could do.

Birdie walked step by step and arm in arm with me along that road to the cemetery of the bombed church. She stood by my side as my nephew's body went into the ground. Today, young folks and newcomers don't understand what the times were like back then, even here in Ridgetop. Birdie and I agreed for both our sakes, and especially Birdie's because she risked the wrath of her own people - we agreed to never speak of it here. That was Miss Birdie Campbell's moment, and though the years may have made her a stubborn old lady in the eyes of some, that moment lives on for me. And now I hope it will live on for you.

That's all I wanted to say . . . except I know God has welcomed her into His arms and the trumpets of glory sounded the moment she entered the Kingdom.

HATTIE stops speaking. The chapel is silent for a few seconds. HATTIE starts to walk away. LILY catches her arm and hugs her.

WINFIELD

Amen, sister Hattie. Amen!

EVERYONE in the chapel stands up and greets one another.

TONIA runs up and hugs HATTIE, then spontaneously hugs ACE. ACE enthusiastically responds.

ACTION FREEZES. LIGHTS DIM

SPOTLIGHT up on Narrator JOHN AGEE

JOHN is standing on opposite wing of stage. He is in narrator wardrobe with hat, fishing pole and a tackle box.

JOHN AGEE

And so Birdie Campbell left our little community with a send-off this town will never forget. And Ace, well, Ace saw there's no life in death unless there's someone who knows our stories. . . someone to connect one generation to the next. We're all just stories wantin' a memory . . . a memorial. Of course, I planned to go back to work. Couldn't leave them flounderin', could I? But I thought I'd take some time off and wait till after Christmas to make my peace with Horace . . . and to tell Ace to follow his own heart like I shoulda done years ago.

Yep, instead of talkin' to them right after Birdie's funeral, I waited . . . and I let a moment slip away from me again.

JOHN looks at his fishing pole and shakes his head.

ACTION continues in chapel as funeral attendees continue greeting, now quietly and somberly. They return to seats.

JOHN

I didn't catch it while I could. So, that's that. I'm done . . . almost. I've just been hanging around waitin' . . . for Now.

Lights up full on chapel set.

Ace is behind the lectern and HATTIE and TONIA are seated on the front row with LILY, HORACE, and BRENDA. An easel is beside ACE. A plaque the size of the one Horace had is on the easel with its back facing mourners and audience.

ACE

(as if joining speech in progress)

And so he's not gone . . . not really. His presence will always be here . . . in this chapel where he helped so many remember the loved ones of their lives. My only regret is I never really told him how much he was loved.

ACE reaches over and turns the plaque around.

ACE

Well, as long as there is a McAdams Funeral Home, the name of John Agee will be part of it. This plaque will always grace the wall of our chapel so that future generations will remember. It reads - "In Memory of John Agee, whose service to others in their hour of grief and sorrow represented the heart and soul of this funeral home for four generations."

ACE looks up to heaven.

                    ACE (cont'd)

John, may your spirit never die.

ALL CHARACTERS except JOHN AGEE freeze. JOHN smiles to theatre audience.

                    JOHN

What a nice surprise. Didn't I say he was a bright bulb? Yep, I missed the year 2000 by one day. One day. But I ain't complainin'. Not bad goin' in your sleep. And I guess I wasn't what they call Y2K ready. That's why I sure am glad y'all are here. Maybe you can tell Hattie and the McAdams for me. Tell 'em . . . tell 'em I love 'em. Well, Ernie's holdin' a fishin' spot for me at the river. I'll be seein' ya. Y'all take care . . . . No, y'all take care of each other, and then I'm sure I'll be seein' ya.

JOHN walks through the frozen chapel scene, softly but audibly singing chorus of "Shall We Gather At The River." He repeats chorus as necessary for action.

                    JOHN (cont'd)

"Yes, we'll gather at the river,

The beautiful, the beautiful river.

Gather with the Saints at the river

That flows by the throne of God."

He stops his walk, but not his singing as he admires the plaque for a few seconds. Then he continues walking into the shadows. ECHO EFFECT on his voice as it fades into oblivion.

Lights fade out

CURTAIN

LYRICS FOR JOHN AGEE'S HYMNS

"Shall We Gather At The River"

- Robert S. Lowry 1864

1.	Shall we gather at the river,
Where bright angel feet have trod,
With its crystal tide forever
Flowing by the throne of God?
CHORUS:
Yes, we'll gather at the river,
The beautiful, the beautiful river,
Gather with the saints at the river
That flows by the throne of God.

2.	On the margin of the river,
Washing up its silver spray,
We will talk and worship ever,
All the happy golden day.
CHORUS:

3.	Ere we reach the shining river,
Lay we every burden down;
Grace our spirits will deliver,
And provide a robe and crown.
CHORUS:

4.	Soon we'll reach the shining river,
Soon our pilgrimage will cease;
Soon our happy hearts will quiver
With the melody of peace.
CHORUS:

"Peace Like a River"   American Traditional

1. I've got peace like a river,
I've got peace like a river,
I've got peace like a river in my soul.
I've got peace like a river,
I've got peace like a river,
I've got peace like a river in my soul.

2. I've got love like a river, . . .

3. I've got joy like a river, . . .

"Amazing Grace" - John Newton (1725-1807)

1. Amazing grace! How sweet the sound
That saved a wretch like me.
I once was lost but now am found,
Was blind but now I see.

2. 'Twas grace that taught my heart to fear,
And grace my fears relieved,
How precious did that grace appear,
The hour I first believed.

3. Through many dangers, toils and snares
I have already come.
'Tis grace hath brought me safe thus far,
And grace will lead me home.

4. When we've been there ten thousand years,
Bright shining as the sun,
We've no less days to sing God's praise
Than when we'd first begun.

"When The Roll Is Called Up Yonder"
- James Milton Black 1893

1. When the trumpet of the Lord shall sound, and

time shall be no more,
And the morning breaks, eternal, bright and fair;
When the saved of earth shall gather over on the other shore,
And the roll is called up yonder, I'll be there.
CHORUS:
When the roll, is called up yonder,
When the roll, is called up yonder,
When the roll, is called up yonder,
When the roll is called up yonder I'll be there.
2. On that bright and cloudless morning when the dead in Christ shall rise,
And the glory of His resurrection share;
When His chosen ones shall gather to their home beyond the skies,
And the roll is called up yonder, I'll be there.
CHORUS:
3. Let us labor for the Master from the dawn till setting sun,
Let us talk of all His wondrous love and care;
Then when all of life is over, and our work on earth is done,
And the roll is called up yonder I'll be there.
CHORUS:

www.ingramcontent.com/pod-product-compliance
Lightning Source LLC
Chambersburg PA
CBHW061336040426
42444CB00011B/2955